Don't Let Your Brain Go Numb

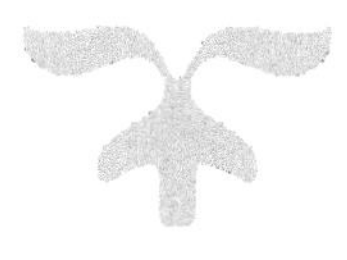

Regaining Power Through Resilience

PRESENT

Don't Let Your Brain Go Numb

Regaining Power Through Resilience

By: *Stacey Bulluck*

Reach The Press Publishing
608 McConnell Court
Middle River, Maryland 21220

Printed in the United States of America

TABLE OF CONTENT

Don't Let Your Brain Go Numb

I was going along on this journey and came to notice that I had no joy, nor did I have the ability to create happiness for myself. My life could have been described using the first stanza of Sade's song "Soldier of Love." The lyrics are, "I've lost the use of my heart, but I'm still alive." My heart had been snuffed out, and I felt helpless and depleted. I was numb. At that time, I didn't have the ability to think, feel, do, or be. I was not in the state of being able. I was just a soldier walking around taking orders from all the behaviors of the people, situations, and things around me. My heart did not move me to fulfill my purpose. I was stuck. Deprived of the power of sensation. No feeling, desensitized, senseless. All I had was the emotional tornado in my life, and it was taking precedence over everything regarding my heart and mind. I was not responsive. I was paralyzed on the inside!

Life will bring its stuff, and I want to help with the process of being prepared when the tornadic winds blow. This book will provide some tools needed for building your permanent plan to fulfill the purpose and help gain a clear understanding about what it will take to become unstuck, walk in freedom and be the prolific human being you were created to be.

We will explore how to combat becoming numb and helpless. Finally, we will gain a powerful understanding of how to avoid returning to our original state, just being dust without form and void. Instead, we discover, learn, how to **BE** in our intended state of manifesting God on earth – which is being a living soul and thriving from the place where life was injected initially.

Let's explore how we can become deprived of feelings and subsequently become paralyzed and unresponsive. It is the goal to get a full understanding of how the brain goes numb. Most important, we will take the time to discover and learn what it takes to bring back feelings, sensitivity, comprehension, and awareness of who we are. With the goal of **BEING** at the forefront. Yes, being who we are. Having actuality, being in total contrast to our original state of being formless and void. I know, I used the word being so many times, but it was on purpose because I need you to understand the severity of this matter. It's monumental! I need you to move successfully through the journey.

Oh, trust me, on this journey you will come to those places along the way designed to stop all forward progress, but you don't have to be worried or concerned because the words on these pages are going to unlock and open the eyes of our understanding. As we receive the spirit of wisdom and revelation, our minds will regain vitality and purpose. All numbness dissipates, and the flood gates of enlightenment are sure to open. The hope of His calling will be well-defined, and the demonstration of what the riches of this glorious birthright means to those of us who believe there is exceeding the greatness of His supremacy toward us. (Ephesians 1: 16-19). You believe it right! Yes, you are destined for greatness! So, come on, let's dig in and see the enormity of the power that is already in you.

Chapter 1

Without Feeling or Sensation

Don't let your brain go numb. Don't let it turn to mush. You cannot allow this to happen. We must fight! We must fight for what was given to us by God. We have been given a life full of God, along with faith, love, perseverance, and gentleness. When you allow your brain to go numb, it is void and does not have the capacity or determination to pursue the truth of who we are. We all have been given a gift which we need to give away while walking the journey. However, some oppositions that come to deter us from sharing our gifts to the fullest. Our gifts can become dormant through life's harmful devices.

The minute the negative devices are given permission by us, to trap us into entertaining our thoughts and producing many foolish and harmful desires that plunge us into ruin and destruction (1 Timothy 6:9) the mind turns to a sloop, goo, and mire. This is clearly not what the brain is meant to do. According to Psychology Today, the primary purpose of a brain is so that we will have a cognitive function and can move around our environment in a meaningful way. That is the psychological purpose, yes, of course, there are physiological reasons too, but for the sake of this book, we will stick with the mental portion. You must not allow your brain to lose its purpose. Notice I used the word allow on purpose. We must not give permission or authorize our own demise.

When something goes numb, it can no longer be used for its intended function. Wow, if we subscribe to the Psychology Today purpose of the brain when it loses its intended purpose, our ability to function dies. Once the planned role has diminished all intent, goals, and objectives may be lost. Allowing this to happen takes away feelings and sensations, and we become desensitized, senseless, and unfeeling towards everything. The good, the bad, and the ugly. This is an open door for the death of dreams, visions, and aspirations. Because you are no longer operating according to what your heart is compelling you to do. At this point, the heart/mind is not giving any instructions at all. Therefore, without guidance, there is no execution.

All our visions come from within our inner man. The place that is the source of who we are. The brain will send a message to the heart, from a neurological standpoint, but it will also send a message from a purposeful, passionate perspective. You were created to have the power to think who you are. However, if the brain is not functioning in its intended role, the heart, the mind of man, will not comprehend what it is being told. Therefore, if the brain is void of feeling and now deadened; your passions, gifts, and talents lay dormant, inactive, and undeveloped. The true spirit of you. The spirit which drives the human. What we see outwardly is not the driver of your soul. Your spirit is the fuel of your soul, which is the place where your mind, will, and intellect produce, but when it is numb, nothing is being heard nor understood.

Proverbs 23:7 As a man thinks in his heart, so is he: Proverbs 4:23 Keep vigilant watch over your heart; that's where life starts.

You must understand the spiritual principles of a spiritual being. Because we are not just the outside container which can be seen; we are so much more. We are spiritual beings created by a Supreme Spirit, and I call him God. There are standards to follow. First, "What you say flows from what is in your heart." Second, "Your true being brims over into true words and deeds." In other words, what you say is what will be produced, but when and if the brain is not in the receptive mode and it's in mush mode, it will not deliver because it does not understand. **Without understanding, it will not send the message to the body, and we are stripped of the power to comprehend, stripped of the ability to realize, and stripped of the power to appropriately respond.**

Matthew 12:34-37 King James Version (KJV)
34 O generation of vipers, how can ye, being evil, speak good things? For out of the abundance of the heart, the mouth speaketh.

35 A good man out of the good treasure of the heart bringeth forth good things: and an evil man out of the evil treasure bringeth forth evil things.

36 But I say unto you, that every idle word that men shall speak, they shall give account thereof in the Day of Judgment.

37 For by thy words thou shalt be justified, and by thy words, thou shalt be condemned.

Chapter 2

Defeating the Opposition and Walking in Fulfillment

1 Corinthian 16:9 There is a wide-open door for a great work here, although many oppose me.

Before we arrived on this scene called earth, the plan was set in motion. We come here having what it will take for us to be successful on the journey. But unfortunately, we may have gotten waylaid along the way and missed instructions on defeating the opposition. The opposition is those things that try and stop us from achieving or at least **try** and prevent us from succeeding. One too many oppositions and the mind begins to retreat shutdown. In other words, the brain goes numb. We do not want to give in to the pressure of resistance. This journey is going to provide opportunities, which I like to call them whose goal fighters, who bring confrontation and cause you to struggle.

The root word of opposition is to oppose. When something or in many cases someone and let me interject here, in most cases that someone is the person you see when you look in the mirror, is in opposition to you it's not you the human it's opposing it's your **BEING**. It opposes the vital force of your true self. What happens when there is a force that is the opposite of vibrant, energetic, and victorious. It then is a resistance made to lie contrary. Do you see where this is going? The opposition has come to rest to you. It is an adversary to who you really are.

I was having a conversation the other day with a childhood friend, and I was talking to her about the person who I was when I left home at 19 years old, to join the military. By that time, we had been friends for about 7 or 8 years. So, she was around to see some very formidable years of my journey. Long story short, I revealed to her I was really mean when at the beginning of my military career. Let me pause here and say, thank, God intervened, and the real me dropped the mean defensive behavior. Ok back to our conversation, I asked her was I mean growing up, and she said: "no, not that she remembered." Trust me if anyone would know my behavior, she would be someone who was a witness. We spent every day together from 12 years old to the day I left at 19 years old.

This told me that somewhere on the journey, I started to believe what I had been exposing as a child. That I was evil and that I was a "black rattlesnake!" I know pretty harsh words to say to a kid right but, back to the principal and essential point, the opposition lied to me. See when resistance speaks, it does not tell the truth. I learned much later on the journey that I must comprehend within this process to resist the lie. That lie was the main culprit trying to abort my purpose, and it came to steal my power of resilience. You see, I have come to learn that being resilient gives vision.

I want to give you an illustration of how resistance to the opposition works if we apply our own resilience. There is a form of exercise called resistance exercise, and it is excellent in achieving and improving muscle strength and tone. You know most of us women want arms that look like "Michelle Obama arms." Insert laughter here. The men some want arms like Dewayne "The Rock" Johnson. Guess what that takes work. Just as it takes work and effort to resist the opposition and win, but you can do it! We are going to gain some new spiritual workouts and develop our spiritual arms so we will be able to protect our ability to **BE** flexible, balanced, and ready to walk in an improved sense of **BEING**. In the natural, this is what the resistance exercise does. It helps to build muscular strength and endurance.

As you grow stronger, you won't get tired as quickly, and the lies of the opposition won't be able to weigh you down. You will not give up the fight and just give in to the continual barrage of everyday life. You'll be able to fight back and withstand the pressure. Why because now you have an improved sense of wellbeing. You are beginning to have a better understanding of who you are. Your spiritual insights are returning, no longer deadened or desensitized. Even the natural human part of your resistance training is boosting your self-confidence, improving your body image and your mood, your sleep is improving; you have increased self-esteem; enhanced performance of everyday tasks. You are ready to move forward and go through the doors that God has prepared for you.

If we want to walk through opened doors, we must be willing to go through what it takes to conquer those that oppose us.

Joshua 1:8-9 The Message (MSG) Don't get off track, either left or right, to make sure you get to where you're going. And don't for a minute let this Book of The Revelation be out of mind. Ponder and meditate on it day and night, making sure you practice everything written in it. Then you'll get where you're going; then you'll succeed. Haven't I commanded you? Strength! Courage! Don't be timid; don't get discouraged. God, your God, is with you every step you take."

Joshua 1:8-9 King James Version (KJV) 8 This book of the law shall not depart out of thy mouth; but thou shalt meditate therein day and night, that thou mayest observe to do according to all that is written therein: for then thou shalt make thy way prosperous, and then thou shalt have good success. 9 Have not I commanded thee? Be strong and of good courage; be not afraid, neither be thou dismayed: for the Lord thy God is with thee whithersoever thou goest.

There is a lesson here to learn from Joshua's experience. True courage is sharpened by the opposition. This was not the time for him to back down. Just like with you and I, this is no time to back down, shut down or be timid. This is the time to take on the opposition because this resistance has only made the reality of who we are come alive. I know for sure, that when we want something bad enough and there is something that tries to get in the way it should only do one thing and that is to make us want it even the more. I call it a catalyst.

Note: Opposition cannot break the spirit of those who want to become and move out of being stuck, numb, and desensitized. Use discord as fuel and encouragement. Allow it to ignite you with fresh courage.

To conquer the opposition, we must have an understanding of what is happening. We have to trust the process. The process may seem a little rough at times, but the end result is that of perseverance, character, and hope. There were times that I allowed the lies told to me about me, to strip my ability to persevere, and it most definitely robbed me of good character. Guess what, I'm here to tell you that you can and will outlast the lies. This is when you gain peace with God and therefore have peace within that is unshakeable. Of course, as you will discover throughout these pages, there is not a day that goes by where you won't be shaken. That is a part of the process. Remember if we just trust the process we win every time. We get to stand in grace and access God, who is the answer to all things. We gained this access by trusting and having confidence in God. And because we are secure, immovable, we can do the great work because we know the opposition is part of the fruit-bearing process.

The ground of your heart may shake as if there is an earthquake, but this is the time when God is removing the barriers that kept us in a dead place. God will tear up everything that has hardened our surroundings just to wake us up from the deadened, desensitized spot we find ourselves in. **ASK THE LORD TO SPLIT THE ROCKS AND OPEN UP THE DOOR OF YOUR TOMB SO YOU CAN COME OUT AND APPEAR TOO MANY.**

Romans 5: 1-4
1Therefore, since we have been justified through faith, we have a feeling of peace with God through our Lord Jesus Christ, 2through whom we have gained access by faith into this grace in which we stand, and we exult in the hope of the glory of God.
3Not only that, but we also rejoice in our sufferings, because we know that suffering produces perseverance; 4perseverance, character; and character, hope.

Matthew 27:51-53 The Message (MSG) 51-53 at that moment, the Temple curtain was ripped in two, top to bottom. There was an earthquake, and rocks were split into pieces. What's more, tombs were opened up, and many bodies of believers asleep in their graves were raised. (After Jesus' resurrection, they left the tombs, entered the holy city, and appeared too many.)

For us to walk through an open door for the purpose of **BEING** whom we truly are not being the lies, we were told. We will have to trust the moments that are meant to build us, build our expectation in God, that He has empowered us.

Paul said there is great work to be done. That tells me we must have exalted expectation that something good will happen. I saw this commercial the other day, and it caught my attention, and I want to share it with you in hopes that it will stick with you as it sticks with me. It's the Duracell motto, and it says, "Trust is Power." Always remember that. Trust in God, so His power will work in and through us. Make trusting the power of God in your regular and not the lies as the standard of who you are.

Chapter 3

This is Not Normal: So Stop Accepting As Such

Have you found yourself feeling as if you were stuck in this journey called life? This may have taken place after suffering a blow to the mind, which I may, at times, interchange with the word heart. Meaning your place of emotions, passions, and your willpower. Many of us have taken multiple blows. On occasion, the misfortunes all came at the same time and or some happened over time, and we became numb to despair and disappointment and began to accept them as the norm. When fear, frustration, physical or emotional pain happens, it becomes challenging to manage thoughts and emotions, things may be overwhelming. When this happens, we have a choice. We can trust the instinct of the fight or flight response, or at a minimum, we should stand up and raise our level of awareness, but when the mind, the heart, the center of humanity has taken mental blows for a very long time the ability to respond is not there. We have accepted this as usual, and for some, it's all they know. This possibly could have begun during childhood. Some parents gave the blows with their belittling words, such as stupid, dumb, or you will never amount to anything. It started with the parent and continued in every relationship after that, why because that was what we had become accustomed to, and this was the norm. The standard if you will, thus the reason for the continual press to find it throughout the journey. We tend to go back to what we knew. Back to the dust and void. Back to nothingness as if that is where we belong. I'm familiar with the low places on the journey, but just because I'm familiar with it, it is not indicative of who I am. Nor does it indicate who you are.

Have you noticed that some of the people around you remind you of what is familiar to you? Hurt, disappointment, and fear are all things that we have experienced on our journey. The last thing we should do is allow these momentary afflictions to numb our minds. Our numbness will turn in to complete destruction if we allow it. It can destroy our ability to grow, develop, mature, and prosper. Well enough of that, I think you get the picture.

These things were sent to break to you. However, I'm going to make a **bold** statement and guarantee if you continue reading and pressing to move forward and not stay stuck, your brain (mind, will, emotions) will be restored. Restoration can happen the minute we accept ourselves as the vessels with treasures and stop seeing ourselves in the story of the world and not our own. Let's bring out your true identity. Let's **BE** the fulfillment of who God, the creator of all declares you to **BE**. Not conformed to the ideas/thoughts of the world of who you are or should be. Not even conform to the belief in your mind that only produce hopelessness and despair. You are necessary. I promise you are. Let's give permission and allow God to transform our spirit, soul, and body. We do not live according to the world's code. We live according to every word that proceeds out of Gods mouth.

Deuteronomy 28:13 Message - God will make you the head, not the tail; you'll always be the top dog, never the bottom dog, as you obediently listen to and diligently keep the commands of God, your God, that I am commanding you today.

Someone else would love to dictate our story. Once the brain (mind, emotions, desires, hunger, cravings, and will) is numb, and without sense, it has lost the ability to function in the capacity it was created to perform in. When the brain is numb, its purpose becomes weakened then you begin to unconsciously consent to the opposition's plan, and the beginning of the dictatorship suppresses who you are supposed to **BE**. This is not normal, and we can no longer accept it to be so. The mind is the place where we receive spiritual living instructions from God, which gives us the power to demonstrate his will on the Earth with our body.

Were you aware that your demonstration had stopped and you were no longer being or doing things in life which bring you joy? Most likely, you did not realize it was happening. You lifted your head one day and discovered the journey was still and you were doing the same mundane day after day after day. Some people are okay with living a life of complacency, but that's not normal. Life should not be one dimensional. No excitement, no get up and go; just a lot of sitting around moping and complaining but doing nothing to fulfill a purpose. Don't let the numbing effect set in. Meaning to be exposed to so much pain, hurt, and disappointment that we become numb to it dismissing or not even noticing it depriving us. We will all encounter pain, but when we are numb, we cannot have the ability to feel, and if we cannot feel we will not fix it. Humanity intends the intent of humans is to have dominion over, our lives are to be filled with greatness, intentionally. Becoming so desensitized to what is our true purpose will cause us to look to humanity, this is including looking at ourselves, and unfortunately, often humans will provide a distorted view and make you think, oh perhaps I'm not supposed to accomplish anything, maybe I'm not supposed to be brilliant and produce greatness. You know all those negatives that blind our mind and causes one-sided thinking. What happens when our one thing keeps coming up wrong, we figure we're not good enough or just not smart enough to get it, and we go numb and stop moving forward. Don't believe the lie! Confront it! I decree we are no longer paralyzed by the numbing of our mind, will, intellect, and emotions. We are now revitalized day by day.

Proverbs 19: 21 There are many devices in a man's heart; nevertheless, the counsel of the LORD, that shall stand.

This reminds us the heart of humanity is always coming up with a plan that seems easy, but truthfully, it leads up to a place of being complacent. Being complacent is not a good place to be if we are walking in purpose. Paul said he learned to be content in the situation he was in and that was his revelation because Paul knew who he was and was fully confident he was walking in the power and demonstration of what God had declared him to be. There is nowhere we find Paul not writing, not visiting, not encouraging, or not directing. He was always moving forward in his call. Please understand I'm not stating that everyone is called like Paul to be an Apostle. I am saying that each and every one of us has a purpose that we must fulfill. It may be writing, being a scientist that discovers the cure for a disease, a nanny that has a gift for successfully working with children. Whatever it is, just do it regardless of what the past has given stick your chest out and commit to "nevertheless," you're going to push through and past.

Philippians 4:13 Message - I've learned by now to be quite content whatever my circumstances. I'm just as happy with little as with much, with much as with little. I've found the recipe for being happy whether full or hungry, hands full or hands empty. Whatever I have, wherever I

am, I can make it through anything in the One who makes me who I am.

That's why in the latter part of the verse it says "nevertheless," meaning just because I'm content does not mean I am complacent. At that moment of contentment, we're just waiting for instructions because there is more God needs us to do. I used the word intentionally. This reminds me of the moment in the bible when Jesus sent two of the disciples ahead and gave them instructions and provided clarity for the opposition because he knew it would come. Just as it will with us while walking along this journey. He made sure that they would have a clear direction. He told them, and I paraphrase, that if anyone tries to stop you from completing your mission, tell them the **"Master needs them!" (Matthew 21:3 Message Bible)**

These same words are for you and me. When someone asks what you are doing because you know not everyone is going to understand the unstuck you. Tell them the Master needs me, and I am following His direction.

We receive purpose, guidance, and direction from God, and the path is continuous. What God has spoken is the only thing that will have us to maintain our upright position on this journey. We are not beat down and bent over anymore. We've been hunched over too long. We have bent over backward too many times for all the wrong reasons. Now is the time to allow the true you to stand up and take charge over old the numb, undeveloped you.

Let's get up, out, and free. You are now a new living being ready to live a life that is not trapped.

Chapter 4

Becoming Stuck, Numb, Feeling Worthless

Several areas of life cause us to become stuck. In my instance, it was multiple traumatic experiences along the way. First, I thought as thinking I was worthless and funny enough, I do not remember making any verbal statements of feeling this way, but my actions said everything. It just came to me as I began to write in the previous sentence, "statements of feeling" of no self-worth, I thought to myself, does no self-esteem have a feeling? No! Why because it's numb already. Not having the ability to evaluate your own worth because you are numb, desensitized to any sense of how amazing you are. This is dangerous and detrimental to your **BEING** the vital force in the earth, which is already declared. The thoughts of greatness you possess were deadened by rejection, fear, and disappointment, which then brought on confusion and produced the spirit of fear, which is what has paralyzed you. Always remember **God did not give us a life of fear, he gave us power, love, and an undamaged mind. (2 Timothy 1:7)** In the Message Bible translation, it says this, **"God doesn't want us to be shy with his gifts, but bold and loving and sensible."** He made us reverence Him when using His gifts. When you are low on self-worth, these are the times when a pit stop along the way is necessary to refuel and get renewed. We have examples here for us. One individual I like in particular is King David, he reminds us that the Most High God created us and even though David has a full gamut of misfortunes where he could have just throw in the towel and gave up he makes the pit stop and realizes it is God who made him just the way he is. This is what we must come to understand. In other words, grasp, grip, appreciate, and absorb the fullness of who we are. In Psalm 139, we have a powerful daily affirmation to make when we get up every day. For real, the renewal comes day by day, so don't get frustrated because this is a daily process.

Psalms 139:14 Thank you for making me so wonderfully complex! Your workmanship is marvelous—how well I know it. (New Living Translation)

How well do you know it? We all make mistakes, have failed attempts, and are disappointed, sometimes by those who are closest to us, but that is no reason to begin the process of giving up. O yes! That is a process too. It wasn't overnight the numbing thoughts, or negatives events happened in our lives. Nope, it happened over time. My prayer is, now that by reading this book, your awareness is being opened and restored, so when the next moment comes, you will have tools to combat the pain. I know depression is never easy, but if we have the right arsenal to fight with, we can deaden the pain by healing it instead of allowing it to anesthetize us.

Do not allow hurt, rejection, or disappointment to rob you or bring your determination to a state of being paralyzed. Let us heal together.

Psalms 147:3 He heals the brokenhearted and bandages their wounds. (New Living Translation)

This tells me that a broken heart should be covered to receive full healing. This will take time. Time doing what staying covered, staying in God's presence. Exposing the wound before it's healed, you're at risks of scabbing, which is a hardened covering instead of soft, pliable skin that is rejuvenated and brand new. When there is a hard scab in its place, this hardened covering could delay healing and increase scarring, and we're still stuck and in pain. Stay in the presence of God period.

Psalms 91: 1 He that dwelleth in the secret place of the most High shall abide under the shadow of the Almighty. 2 I will say of the LORD, He is my refuge and my fortress: my God; in him will I trust.

My prayer is Gods healing bandage will allow your wounds to fully heal, and while you are covered any other possibilities of being injured in this same area will be canceled. Let's stay safe in a secret place.

Chapter 5

A Clouded Mind - Sure-Fire Way to Open the Wound Again

Being numb to life will cause you to take on things that are out of your control. Because you cannot feel the weight, you believe it's not too heavy for you. Numbness will make you believe that you can control it. Unfortunately, being void of physical and emotional feeling can put us in a state of delusion, and that only breeds misunderstanding and misconceptions. Our mind is not in focus, but rather it is like a camera out of focus, all blurry and stuff. Our ideas become foggy, the brain is cloudy and crowded, which throws off our ability to make sound decisions. I strongly encourage you to take notice when it becomes challenging to make decisions, I mean sensible, rational choices.

Because we cannot make a concrete decision, we begin to take on everything as if we are superhuman. This only causes more pain. Piling more things on our plate doesn't make the pain go away; it just causes more numbing. You know what happens when you carry something for too long when you put it down you find that your arm is numb and now you must shake it until the feeling comes back. Piling things will only make it harder to use the limb properly, and not only does it affect its functionality; it also affects how long it takes for the numbness to go away. The more you pile, the heavier it gets and the longer we go through motions of bringing back feeling. Now that is a physical limb, we can't or shouldn't physically shake our brains. Nor can we shake the mind on our own.

We must spiritually have our mind transformed. Let me suggest first, not to take on more than we can handle. Perhaps there are things that physically you can control with no problem, but in this instance, I am referring to emotionally and spiritually not to take on more than we can handle.

What do you mean spiritually and emotionally? From a spiritual standpoint, it is possible to start using spirituality as an escape from the issues of mortal life. For example, it is possible to find yourself at every event the church has or activities that should enhance your spiritual growth, but it's a cover-up for the pain. We sometimes do things in the name of Jesus, but it has no power, and it only hinders us because we are not willing to expose the real issue of being hurt, disappointed, discouraged and rejected. We have now created a church mask. Also, if we are attending every event, that is now a financial burden. It takes gas to drive, you need money for the offering. Oh, and don't forget going out to eat afterward. You know I'm telling the truth. It's ok you can go ahead and laugh here. By doing and going it's possible now the finances needed to maintain the household are used on external events. Another way the neglect of the home starts to show perhaps with dirty laundry stacked to the ceiling or the mailbox is filled with past due and cut off notices. I'm not saying for you not to attend. However, I am saying make sure you are not overwhelming yourself versus being your sensible self and knowing what you can and cannot take on at this phase of the journey.

To be emotionally overwhelmed can produce feelings of loneliness and shame. It is possible to be overcome by the constant waves of demonstrative drives and become over-stimulated when things are too chaotic for a long time. This can lead to psychological wounding. We must understand there are times we will be "among wolves," and this requires greater use of wisdom.

Matthew 10: 16 Behold, I am sending you out as sheep in the midst of wolves, so be wise as serpents and innocent as doves.

It is necessary to make wise choices. Of course, God wants us to help when and where we can, however, if you cannot take on another thing, please don't. It will only hurt not help. Stay in your lane, understand your gift or gifts. For example, I know I'm a writer and a teacher. So, guess what

I'm going to the choir director asking to lead a solo. That would overwhelm me and cause me to retreat. Retreating or withdrawing is a sign of numbing.

In one of my favorite scriptures, Romans 12: 1 God asks that we take our every day, "ordinary life—your sleeping, eating, going-to-work, and walking-around life—and place it before God as an offering." (Message Translation) Everything about us is brought as a contribution to daily life. This certainly makes life much more comfortable. We don't have to worry about who we are pleasing daily. Your only option is to please your Creator. It merely allows, God, to direct your path and order your steps; this will keep us from piling on too much. When our life is turned over to him, he is the one carrying everything. He has promised to help us to be balanced and not overburdened. Don't become such a great imitator of society that you fit into it without even thinking. Instead, the solution is to focus your mind on God. You'll be changed from the inside out. We want to stay free of heavy loads and unnecessary stress. Stay free of the need to take on too many things in life. Take on the matters the Lord gives, he is aware of how much you can handle. Just like the architect and builder of the elevator, they know how much weight it can hold. They use specific materials which have proven their capacity. I pray that we will follow the wise instruction given to us in Proverbs and Romans.

Romans 12:1-2 The Message (MSG) Place Your Life Before God 12 1-2 So here's what I want you to do, God helping you: Take your everyday, ordinary life—your sleeping, eating, going-to-work, and walking-around living—and place it before God as an offering. Embracing

what God does for you is the best thing you can do for him. Don't become so well-adjusted to your culture that you fit into it without even thinking. Instead, fix your attention on God. You'll be changed from the inside out. Readily recognize what he wants from you, and quickly respond to it. Unlike the culture around you, always dragging you down to its level of immaturity, God brings the best out of you, develops well-formed maturity in you.

Proverbs 3: 5-6 Trust God from the bottom of your heart; don't try to figure out everything on your own. Listen for God's voice in everything you do, everywhere you go; he's the one who will keep you on track. Don't assume that you know it all. Run to God! (Message Translation)

Chapter 6

Desensitized

When the voice of pain stripped me of my ability to hear and comprehend clearly, it removed all feeling of importance. Once importance is removed from the human psyche, we become so desensitized to the inner voice that we're supposed to hear, the view which propels us forward and gives step by step instructions along the path. Instead, the numbness has blocked our internal hearing, which has affected our understanding, and now there is a disconnect. That disconnect causes the passion for pursuing anything, let alone seek God, becomes silenced and deadened. **Do not become the extinguisher of your Passion.**

Let's pray and believe that God will continue to open the eyes of our understanding, because, at this point, pain, rejection, and disappointment are competing to overrule our ability to feel. BUT (Believers Understanding Truth) know that it is God who will show us the way out of the darkness and into the place where we are exposed by his light. This means we no longer hide the pain, rejection, and disappointment it is exposed for healing in the presence of God.

Psalm 3:3 - But thou, O LORD, [art] a shield for me; my glory, and the lifter up of mine head.

There are those times in life when the mental clutter makes it is difficult to hear, BUT God has the plan airtight, and if we choose abundance while on the journey, the path is lit.

Just follow the light, you may not be able to see the entire way but trust it, and the more you believe, the more the feeling and hearing will return. Feeling of discerning the next move and hearing the voice to follow. No longer desensitized of the most critical voice the only sound that can cause mountains to move and the entire world to open for you.

Proverbs 3:5-12 (Message Translation) Trust God from the bottom of your heart; don't try to figure out everything on your own. Listen for God's voice in everything you do, everywhere you go; he's the one who will keep you on track. Don't assume that you know it all. Run to God! Run from evil! Your body will glow with health, your very bones will vibrate with life! Honor God with everything you own; give him the first and the best. Your barns will burst, your wine vats will brim over. But don't, dear friend, resent God's discipline; don't sulk under his loving correction. It's the child he loves that God corrects; a father's delight is behind all this.

My prayer is that we open up and allow God to replace and restore our numbness – desensitization to full circulation back to the Master's default setting. Where we are free to move, live, and have our being (Acts 17:28). These words from Isaiah give us an expected end to what we will receive when trusting God to move for us and turn his way into our new normal. The new normal being able to receive roses, feel joy, rejoice, and win a new title as an Oak tree, established explicitly to show off for God who is going to give you double for your trouble!

Isaiah 61:3 (Message Translation) To care for the needs of all who mourn in Zion, give them bouquets of roses instead of ashes, Messages of joy instead of news of doom, a praising heart instead of a languid spirit. Rename them "Oaks of Righteousness" planted by God to display his glory. They'll rebuild the old ruins, raise a new city out of the wreckage. They'll start over on the ruined cities, take the rubble left behind and make it new. You'll hire outsiders to herd your flocks and foreigners to work your fields, But you'll have the title "Priests of God," honored as ministers of our God. You'll feast on the bounty of nations, you'll bask in their glory. Because you got a double dose of trouble and more than your share of contempt, Your inheritance in the land will be doubled, and your joy goes on forever.

Chapter 7

The Transformation Begins and Forever Evolves

God will use all five human senses for the transformation. Once we make the decision to change our mind and cry out for a renewal of the heart, the place where all of life's matters flow from. The process to remove ourselves from the emotional tornado starts here.

Romans 12:1-3 (Gods Word Translation) I encourage you to offer your bodies as living sacrifices, dedicated to God and pleasing to him. This kind of worship is appropriate for you. 2 Don't become like the people of this world. Instead, change the way you think. Then you will always be able to determine what God really wants—what is good, pleasing, and perfect. 3b Your thoughts should lead you to use *good judgment* based on what God has given each of you as believers.

We sometimes find ourselves in tornadic disarray, which is only located in our mind. It seems as if nothing brings rest or peace. It seems all is a spinning funnel of thoughts and feelings. Many which are disordered and confused. The minute you discover this is taking place, at that very moment stop and reach for your instead tool. Say it out loud, **I'm pulling out my tool of changing the way I think about this situation and any other situation/circumstance that does not bring peace.** Yes, life is going to bring some stuff our way. There is no way to get around or out of it. We live in these mortal bodies, which are subject to human tendencies. However, if you learn this vitally important lesson, it will serve you well throughout your life.

Tell yourself that you are changing your perspective. Say, I refuse to adapt to anything that is going to take me off the path already determined for me. I call it having an alternative view. When I mentored young women, who were incarcerated, I would tell them it is a must that we have an alternative to the negative things we were once accustomed to. Our choice was and still is a life of worship, and no, I do not mean we sit and sing slow songs about God all day, but we live a life that respects and honors God. No, I'm not saying that nothing will come your way when you reverence God. The prime example is Jesus. He lived his life reverencing God the Father, and he was beaten and bruised, hung and left to die, but that was his purpose, the work he came to do here on earth. What I am saying, is that even though he went through all those things in his flesh, his spirit was elevated, and he was able to complete his purpose. During this 33-year process, he was able to push through the emotional disappointment, hurt, pain, and fear and win! I know, I know some may say Jesus did not have these earthly issues, but yes, he did Hebrews makes us aware of this.

Hebrews 4:15-16 We don't have a priest who is out of touch with our reality. He's been through weakness and testing, experienced it all—all but the sin. So let's walk right up to him and get what he is so ready to give. Take the mercy, accept the help. (Message Bible Translation)

This is our goal to complete the process. To get to the end where we can say it is "finished," get to the finish line as a WINNER! I heard someone say, but we are not at the end, and my friend, you're exactly right. I'm still alive, and Jesus died, but the good news is He showed us how to get up again and this time with power. So, we cannot give up midway or allow our mind, will, emotions, passion, and purpose to be cut off before completion. Say this with me, **I'm going to fight to the end and never give up because I am not finished. I am making a conscious effort to alter my thoughts and to use good judgment based on what I know God has given me to do. I no longer operate with a commonplace mentality, but I am running to win, and I operate with a precise aim moving toward the goal of my expected end, which is filled with hope for my future.**

Philippians 3:12 GOD'S WORD Translation (GW) It's not that I've already reached the goal or have already completed the course. But I run to win that which Jesus Christ has already won for me.

Jeremiah 29:11 Common English Bible (CEB) I know the plans that I have for you, declares the Lord. They are plans for peace and not disaster plans to give you a future filled with hope.

Chapter 8

Follow the Blueprint

Now that we are free, we must remain free, so we can get to the future, which is filled with hope. When there is hope, there is confidence when there is confidence, there is assurance. We want to continually achieve; therefore, it is necessary to follow the plan designed by God for you and me. Because, we are all unique and wonderfully made, each of us has our own predetermined outcomes, the basic plan is the same, achieving the greatest of self-actualization - the achievement of one's talents and future successes. However, the roads we travel to get there are different. That's why we can't look at another person's life and think we can follow them.

Their path just might take us so far off course that we don't find our way, and for us to reach our intended destinations, it is absolutely necessary to follow your own mapped out a plan. See in society today we have so many options of how to get somewhere. You can use Waze, Google map, Uber, or Lyft, and these may take you in a different direction, and there are times when we take different routes because there are detours along the way. I remember one summer I was following my cousin to a family event, and on my GPS screen it said, "I've found a better route, and it will save you 15 minutes." Well at this point I can still see my cousin in the yellow Corvette she was driving, and I thought she was going to turn at the exit where I was instructed to go, but she didn't and as the directions stated I arrived at our destination about 15 minutes earlier. For whatever the reason the system she used placed her on the route where there was an accident. However, for me, I bypassed the accident altogether. We have to know that some of those detours we may not be prepared for. I have met individuals along the way and asked God how they got so far off the path. He said to me the detour was too much for them to handle, and over time they became numb. The numbing effect killed every desire and ambitious thought. When you are what I call overexposed to the negative ills of life, it eventually your emotions numb themselves to the condition. This is what happens when someone is a victim of repeated molestation, oppression, abuse, etc. Finally, their feelings shut off and are no longer triggered by that negative stimulus and the ability to invoke your fight or flight physiological response is dead. If I can interject here and say the next portion of this book, # 8, we explore how over time how life becomes a norm. Therefore, # 8 helps with the discussion of stopping the rationale that a situation of degradation and pain is normal. No, everyone's routine is not the same. However, it is not healthy for humanity to become desensitized to rejection, hurt, anger, and pain because they have endured it so long; the thought is this must be okay, and that is far from the truth. Yes, we are going to have problems on this journey, but there is an answer IF meaning (if the event that) you are following the blueprint. This journey we're on we win! That's why it's best for us to seek God the Creator of humanity for direction. The Maker knows what direction to take you. However, there are rules to follow. We must keep away from people, places, and things that have a numbing effect. This means there has been so much exposure we no longer notice the damage being done, and it is allowed to take root in the brain as standard.

1 Corinthians 10:13 The Message (MSG) 13 No test or temptation that comes your way is beyond the course of what others have had to face. All you need to remember is that God will never let you down; he'll never let you be pushed past your limit; he'll always be there to help you come through it.

Romans 12:12 The Message (MSG) Be alert servants of the Master, cheerfully expectant. *Don't quit in hard times*; pray all the harder.

Proverbs 3:5-8 The Message (MSG)Trust God from the bottom of your heart; don't try to figure out everything on your own. Listen for God's

voice in everything you do, everywhere you go; he's the one who will keep you on track. Don't assume that you know it all. Run to God! Run from evil! Your body will glow with health, your very bones will vibrate with life!

Second Timothy instructs us to depart from a lifestyle that produces numbness. Instead, we are to stay a vital life force and leave behind the things that caused us to go numb in the first place. We must be purged of allowing things that easily cause us to revert to the days of using only our natural or carnal senses. Instead, we are to use our spiritual knowledge as the primary guide and not solely the human senses. Do not accept anything which denies your life and causes you to become meaningless in your own mind. As a replacement, we must go through the continual process of having a renewed mind. After that, God has promised we will be a vessel unto honor, sanctified, be a light for the Master's use, and prepared unto every good work.

2 Timothy 2:21 New King James Version (NKJV)
21 Therefore if anyone cleanses himself from the latter, he will be a vessel for honor, [a]sanctified and useful for the Master, prepared for every good work.

Hopefully, you desire to be God's design on the earth. To get this accomplished St. John chapter 15 verse 2 declares: in the latter portion of the verse, that every branch that produces, that fulfills its purpose, God continually trims to ensure production of more fruit; do not stop when the pain comes; pruning is not pain free, the process is constant. It is the process of cutting away things that are dead or will cause something to become deadened. The purpose of cutting away is to increase the ability to grow and be fruitful. If we do not allow pruning then we will walk around with dead things hanging on to us, and it is stinky but, if we willingly submit to pruning, it optimally will lead us to sanctification then to elevation. I know that word, sanctification, is not eagerly used today. Please don't view this word as something religious. It is more than that. Sanctification is the vehicle which drives us to the destination that has been mapped out by God. If you want to travel the road which is paved follow the words of Job in chapter 42 verse 2, no thought or purpose of God's can be restrained or thwarted. God has placed a demand on us to be profitable in the earth. So, He is going to use what is necessary to get this done, and in getting it done, fortunately, because God is love, this is done voluntarily. God will not override the human will. However, if we freely make a choice to follow the pain of the cutting away is absorbed by Him. What I mean here is that the emotional pain is absorbed in God's love for you and me.

David was the example when he asked God to purge him with hyssop then create in him a clean heart.

Today, we still need to have our hearts cleaned up. In verse 2 in Psalms 51, David asked God to wash him through and through. The key phrase in this verse is, cleanse me from **my** wickedness. David was not trying to cast blame on anyone; he was willing to take responsibility for his wrong. Are we willing to acknowledge our falling short? God says we must be willing and obedient so we can be partakers of the good land He has prepared for us. God wants to break up any uncultivated ground that has caused a hardening of the heart and numbing of the mind that keeps us from the desire to do His good pleasure.

Isaiah 1:19-20 The Message (MSG) "If you'll willingly obey, you'll feast like kings. But if you're willful and stubborn, you'll die like dogs." That's right. God says so.

How does the ground get broken? Good question! This happens in the storms of life. The ups and downs of life's experience will provide a mechanism to soften the soil and break-up the uncultivated ground and cause it to become the recipient of some much-needed fertilizer from God. That fertilizer is the Spirit of God, which is holy. Therefore, we refer to Him as the Holy Spirit. According to Kathy LaLiberte, "plants need to be fertilized because most soil does not provide the essential nutrients required for optimum growth. Even if you are lucky enough to start with great garden soil, as your plants grow, they absorb nutrients and leave the soil less fertile." So, here it is with humanity, we need essential nutrients to make sure we reach our maximum potential. We all come here with everything we need. We know that fertilizer is required, but no one wants to collect it or spread it out evenly in the soil of our heart, so it can work best. After proper fertilization, seeds of righteousness can be planted. Finally, my brothers and sisters, be strong in the Lord, the stench of the fertilizer will only last for a moment.

2 Peter 1:3 New Life Version (NLV) 3 He gives us everything we need for life and for holy living. He gives it through His great power. As we come to know Him better, we learn that He called us to share His own shining-greatness and perfect life.

Chapter 9

Developing A New Normal

To stop the numbness, you must keep the momentum going. As soon as you get the tingling sensation, you know that feeling you get when you sense the circulation is coming back. Almost everyone I know has experienced numbing either when you sit too long, and your legs or the lower half of your legs go numb. Some of you may be too young to understand this concept, but just keeping on moving forward on the journey and time will have a way of making it happen. Insert smile here! Yes, you smile! Now, the next time you know not to sit too long. You learn, and hopefully, once we are educated on certain things, we no longer do what was done in the past.

We have developed a new pattern to follow. It is straightforward, just to start moving. Moving in the direction of your dreams, goals, and passions. Doing what it will take. For myself, I had to pick up and move from one coast to another.

Heeeyy…check this out though, moving wasn't the hard part. The hard part is keeping the agreement I made with myself and God. I've recently come to realize that I kept arrangements with others more than I keep with myself. I had to become just as important to myself as I was to keep my word to others. I said all that to say when we set new goals, to make sure you keep your promise with yourself.

Ok now back to when your heart/mind gets that feeling of circulation. You know the little tingly feeling that comes back to your fingers after you hit your funny bone, which there is nothing funny about it.

Everywhere I searched to find how to improve circulation; it provided steps of things that should be done consistently. None of the instructions gave a one-step quick-fix. Some had six steps, some twelve, and so on. This just let me know there is no temporary remedy or solution or a one-way fix all. We are each unique and require specific treatment. It is a process. Someone once said, “Rome was not built in a day.” A new normal must be **completed, confirmed, strengthened, and established.** This is the process of making us who we are. We have to do our part in following the procedure. Participating in the process is going to take working continually.

1 Peter 5:10 Amplified 5 After you have suffered for a little while, the God of all grace [Who imparts His blessing and favor], who called you to His own eternal glory in Christ, will Himself complete, confirm, strengthen, and establish you [making you what you ought to be].

Developing a new normal is going to take discipline. Once the flow of creativity returns, we must use control first to choose the direction to head first. Yes, all our goals are lovely; however, it is difficult to manage multiple tasks in the beginning and at the end, for that matter, if it's too much, it's too much. We shouldn't feel responsible for everything, therefore promoting taking on everyone's needs. **You have needs also.** Again, something else I heard someone say, "If we take on too much at the same time, something will get slighted." There may be a temptation to move in a lot of directions at one time. I know how I can sometimes think, especially if one thing doesn't work, then I'm ready to quit everything. Thank God my quitting days are over, and I declare so are yours! We don't want to overwhelm ourselves and then we're back to numbness of mind. We want to commit to that which we are purposed to do at this moment in time. For this season. Aiming at the purpose of developing a habit, it is essential to continually press until the goal is reached.

We are required to become an athlete who strives to win the gold in the Olympics. He or she has a regimented diet, they bring their bodies under subjection to what it will take to have success. We must develop our mind to have a clear focus and

will it to want to win. Guaranteed, when we are obedient to our purpose and follow the path set, you will feast like kings (Isaiah 1:19). Just like me sitting here typing away on this keyboard. If I did not sit and carve out time to express my thoughts, this book would not exist, and without developing a new routine, things just don't pop into being. We are human beings for a reason. God made us human, even he has to follow the rules he put in place. Humans are necessary for the earth realm. But my friend's humans are more significant than just flesh and bones. We have a living spirit within and prayerfully you have chosen to live for the God who breathed and continually provides breath for us to have being, which is significant because this is our origin and there is a result. The result is when passion, desire, and purpose come alive. I know what you are thinking since almighty God breathed being into me how did my brain go numb? I get it, it's hard when you have no desire to be who you are because of the emotional tornado but this question is a good one, but the answer is simple it was a pain, hurt, and disappointment, came to kill the being. **It gave its best effort, but today I declare you have circulation and a fresh creative start in your mind, your will, and your emotions and you are committed to developing new standards that push you beyond any and all pain, hurt, and disappointment.**

Chapter 10

Focused for Purpose

The human spirit is most vigorous when it's focused. When we can center our attention, this demonstrates the mind is functioning correctly, divinely, inspirationally, and cohesively because it's connected to that which created it. It works to the highest capacity in its most intensive frame of mind. This frame of mind or way of thinking renews the human spirit, the being part.

It is an absolute must that we observe and keep our mind/heart. Be sure to carefully examine what is being held in your heart, this will save the place where determination lives (your brain). It is necessary to always guard your heart against allowing negative destroying words to get stored there. We will accomplish this by having a dedicated lifestyle. Being meticulous about what we allow to come in and go out. We can set our mind on the things that show God in the earth. Because after all, we are a spiritual being, and God is Spirit who has exhaled into us the gale force winds of change in our lives. God is skillfully blowing his energy deep within you, eagerly working in you what will give him the most pleasure. Preparing you for the development of his greatness in you. As he prepares us and provides an understanding of what he wants us to do can only be accomplished through an open heart. A heart/mind that desires Gods plan. Knowing what is taking place opens our understanding and the more we know, the more we will do good, kind things for others. It is our responsibility to hold on to this vigor we received during the daily renewal process. His great strength keeps us going no matter what happens—always full of the joy of the Lord. **Scream it to the mountain top RESILIENCE is strong in me!**

How do we maintain that joy we are so full of? Like this, "Forget about what's happened; don't keep going over old history. Be alert, be present." God is doing a brand-new thing in our minds and lives. It's bursting out! Don't you see it?

Isaiah 43:18-19 The Message (MSG) Forget about what's happened; don't keep going over old history. Be alert, be present. I'm about to do something brand-new. It's bursting out! Don't you see it? There it is!

See the vision with your heart and your mind until you see it on earth in physical form. Habakkuk 2 tells us in the Message Version "This **vision**-message is a witness pointing to what's coming. It aches for the coming—it can hardly wait! And it doesn't lie. If it seems slow in coming, wait. It's on its way. It will come right on time." Having an awareness of what God is showing you, it gives us the capacity to move on to the next part of the journey. Because as we follow Gods spirit (His presence), there will always be something new spoken to the human mind.

Proverbs 4:23-27 The Message (MSG) Keep vigilant watch over your heart; that's where life starts. Don't talk out of both sides of your mouth; avoid careless banter, white lies, and gossip. Keep your eyes straight ahead; ignore all sideshow distractions. Watch your step, and the road will stretch out smooth before you. Look neither right nor left; leave evil in the dust.

When you hold on to the presence of God, and you live a determined, diligent lifestyle, keeping your mind on the ways of God. Goodness and mercy will be with you all the days of your life. Let us not become like a dog who returns to its vomit. Stay in the secret place and develop. Remember, you are no longer dead; you are a vital force in the earth. No more walking drenched in shame or guilt. You are focused on purpose.

My prayer is what James speaks to us in chapter one of his book. That when we find ourselves under pressure, "our faith-life is exposed and brought to the forefront and shows its true colors. This way we won't try to get out of anything prematurely, but we allow the working of God in us do its work, and we stay on the path of being mature and well-developed, not deficient in any way." Simply because we make a daily conscious effort to preserve that which is our actuality.

In psychology, our actuality is called self-actualization. It's listed in what is described as Maslow's Hierarchy of Needs. According to the Google dictionary, it means "the realization or fulfillment of one's talents and potentialities, especially considered as a drive or need present in everyone." So even researchers of the mind recognize this drive is in everyone. When you find yourself in the truth of who you never stop reaching. Because there is a well of treasure with unlimited gifts and talents just waiting to be released and someone is waiting for your release.

Knowing that, please understand that I am not telling you this release comes easy. Most of the time when there is an act of releasing, often times it can feel like a significant sacrifice, mainly because we don't know what's going to happen next. It's almost as if coming to the realization of who we are is a scary thing. Most of us haven't seen this person before. I learned in my times of what I like to call stuck-ed-ness or numbness that when the feelings returned, they all came back. That means I was able to feel the pain of what made me fall prey to the numbing effect in the first place, but now **my focus is different**. Go ahead and say that right now. **My focus is different!** I'm not focusing on the pain I'm using the pain as a catalyst to propel me forward. Even if I can't see it or understand where the path is leading. We must trust that what we do not comprehend because it is hidden meaning just because you can't see it and touch with human senses this has no significance because you are not motivated by what your natural eye can see. Instead, you intend to fulfill the purpose and never allow the circumstances of this journey to blind your inherent abilities to have a vision. It's as if this force field so powerful but at the same time gentle and loving overrides the pain now, and you know there is a purpose for all of this. Imagine you can feel it, almost taste it, I realize this may cause my natural senses to be shaken, but the feeling of excitement and overwhelming spiritual sense compels your spirit to seek, ask and knock. Eventually, the full purpose will be revealed, and that revelation makes all desires of flesh meaningless in the heavenly dimensions of God. I believe this is the mindset, character, or attitude if you will, that Jesus had when he was in the garden of Gethsemane, a place that would cause him agony but, he knew he had to do it for the reason of fulfilling a purpose. No, I am not saying that there will be a pain to the degree of death, but then again, some things have to die before something can grow. However, thank God, we don't have to do over what has already been done, but now we are the living sacrifice. To having the ability to understand, causing us to withstand and fight for a purpose.

Chapter 11

Purpose in Crushing Human Tendency

Philippians 3:7-11 GOD'S WORD Translation

7 These things that I once considered valuable, I now consider worthless for Christ. 8 It's far more than that! I consider everything else worthless because I'm much better off knowing Christ Jesus, my Lord. It's because of him that I think of everything as worthless. I threw it all away in order to gain Christ 9 and to have a relationship with him. This means that I didn't receive God's approval by obeying his laws. The opposite is true! I have God's approval through faith in Christ. This is the approval that comes from God and is based on faith 10 that knows Christ. Faith knows the power that his coming back to life gives and what it means to share his suffering. In this way, I'm becoming like him in his death, 11 <u>with the confidence that I'll come back to life from the dead.</u>

The demonstration of what Jesus went through was for the sole purpose of destroying the dead things in life. Earthly, carnal needs and activities are worthless when desiring to fulfill a spiritual purpose. Focusing on these needs will numb, deadened, desensitize, rob us of the power to be fully alive (actualized - "the realization or fulfillment of one's talents and potentialities, especially considered as a drive or need present in everyone").

We must get to the place in life where earthly gain means absolutely nothing. Most often, these gains are a huge distraction and will not provide substance for the journey. There were times in my life when I made a choice to follow diversion, and it cost. It almost cost me the very essence of who I am. Distractions bring all the ill's we have discussed, disappointment, hurt, rejection. This price is too high. We must dismiss the perverted ways of the world in our heart. The Bible describes the heart of man to be wicked, and we learn from Paul in Romans that there is no good thing within us. So, all that we count and depend on an increase, accumulation, or advantage from a worldly perspective, which is temporal, must be brought to nothing in our hearts and minds. When we trust in what the world is offering, we say to God, I don't believe what you have for me. All that has been exalted against the knowledge of God, I implore you to bring it into captivity. Bring it to the secret place of God where corruptible is turned into incorruptible. Bring it to the place where hearts are renewed, and minds are changed from disobedient to obedient, from stone to flesh. Bring it to the area of sacrifice, the place of crushing.

In Philippians chapter 3 verse 8, Paul declares that his earthly gain is useless; there is no expectation of the profit. Now, after you have fought to stay focused, fought with intensity and force. The last thing you want to happen is to get pulled back to the former state of numbness.

Our earthly accomplishments do not amount to a hill of beans in God's kingdom. These so-called attributes are a distraction from the real kingdom commission. Our example is Jesus; He did not allow the impurities of worldly gain, tarnish his purpose. We may desire something so terribly wrong for us that we are willing to sacrifice our mission and give in. DO NOT! I highly encourage you; do not go back. Dig in! You are resilient, I'm going to ask you to continually read, meditate on the resilience chapter. Remember, you have a purpose that has already been determined and planned out. When you start to fill the circulation better known as ideas, wants, and desires, arise in your mind understand this is God renewing your mind and urging you to come, come and accomplish things which have been determined in advance. However, just because they are defined in advance does not mean they are going to automatically appear. They have to be brought out into **BEING**. You are required to develop and nurture your gifts before they are revealed.

Jesus continually gave reminders that He came to fulfill the decree spoken in the heavenly. The course was set, and He did not allow earthly distractions to ruin the plan, which was already decreed. Jesus, a yielded servant, came to the time when His human mission would be fulfilled. The scriptures declare in Luke chapter 22, verses 39-46, Jesus went to a place where He often went, which is called Mount Olivet. Take a closer look; He went to the site when He knew that the time had come for the final crushing of His flesh. Jesus went to a site, not merely a physical location, but a holy place, the place where He would be strengthened to endure the crushing. The scripture clearly denotes that the angel immediately came to give him strength. Once you get to the place of surrender and your mundane task are being done, and you feel as if you cannot do it allow the power of your angels to arise in you. **Never give up!** This is the place where you will be stretched to the end.

The scriptures declare that Jesus became sorrowful and troubled. Because He was in human form, his flesh reacted to the thought of this agonizing task. Just as you and I do when we know there is something significant for us to accomplish and have no idea how it's going to turn out. You know the questions we ask, all the what's, when's, and how's. Although he started His night in the Garden of Gethsemane, meaning "oil press." This is the place or state of mind where we gain the substance needed to fulfill a purpose. He had to go to Gethsemane to receive the anointing for the task ahead, but the process wasn't finished there he had to go further. He had to go up to Mount Olivet, the place of his ascension. Ask God to lead you to your place of ascension to the purpose of producing and go there consistently, so we can have a consistent devotion. This journey is forever growing and developing. We are forever reaching the state of actualization. Discovering all the layers. Unlocking the billions of sensory stimuli's that increase our imagination.

The scripture says Jesus went there often; this is a testament to those of us who are willing to reach, ready to go the distance of the prepared mission; it demands going there often; going, striving, and pressing to attain the prize of knowing intimately the call (the command to execute) of God in you.

The gift of walking in obedience even when you know the result is the death of the flesh (the substance of what the world is offering).

You are drawing near to a place of crushing hurt, pain, disappointment, and rejection. Do not be discouraged because you can feel now, the numbness is no longer there. It's okay to feel. What is important is what we do with our new sense of feeling. Your new sensitive, responsive mind now enables you to embrace the intended plan.

The next time hurt, pain, disappointment, or rejection show up at the door of your heart, look it at from this new perspective with a clear and functioning mind no longer deprived of sensation, no longer rendered useless. No longer destitute of purpose, but **NOW** you are ready to act.

Prepared to achieve. Eager to successfully attain/reach the goal that is set for you. Always remember, greater is God who is in you than he who speaks the things of this cold and malicious world.

Chapter 12

Never Stop Reaching

Hopefully, at this point, you realize that the goal of the enemy was to get you to stop reaching. The trick was to get you to stop **BEING**. Imagine your mind is not capable of having effective communication with your body, and you can no longer tell your arms to reach for what you want. You can see the cookies on the top shelf, but your body just won't cooperate. Well, this is what the enemy wanted to happen spiritually, emotionally, and physically. Even when the natural object seems out of reach, we do what is necessary to get to it. We jump, tiptoe, or get something to stand on, but when the mind is numb, it no longer provokes us to function or move with or in purpose. We just sit there without having any response or reaction.

The goal of reaching or in the spiritual sense being stretched means that we are looking to obtain, to acquire what we truly desire in our heart. Sometimes we will work longer hours reaching to earn more money or notoriety on the job. However, for the purpose of this book, we understand how not to allow our minds to go numb, which stops the desire to attain what we are created to **BE**. Therefore, our reach is focused towards things that may not be physically seen yet, there is an outward display of its inward effect shown through the fruit gained. We have a hope inside us that is pushing us to manifest the truth of our new heart issues. We want to do what is right, we want to be excellent and as eminent as we feel in our inner man. We must keep pushing and developing what we know is the truth of who we are. I'm vague to a certain extent here because I don't know what God has spoken to you or what your passions are. I just know without a doubt there is a greatness in you that someone is waiting for so they can achieve their greatness we all need each other. So, come on, don't stop reaching continue building and reinforcing you're the real you. Your gift is ready to make room for you.

Proverbs 18: 16 A man's gift maketh room for him and bringeth him before great men. King James version.

Reaching it strengthens our physical muscles. Think of reaching and stretching your inner man, stretching and reaching for the goal and prize of purpose. Physical stretching enhances our mobility. If stretching is not done regularly, the muscles become tight and prevent free movement of the body's joints. Unfortunately, I have experienced this physical problem because of an injury sustained while I was in the military. My range of motion is physically impaired, and I had to go to physical therapy many times over to learn stretching techniques to bring back vigor and maneuverability. These stretching exercises must be done consistently. If not done, I can physically feel the tightening of my muscles, and I know that if I make a choice not to stretch the next stop is, I would endure pain and numbness to my limbs.

Isaiah 40: 28 Have you not known? Have you not heard, that the everlasting God, the Lord, the Creator of the ends of the earth, does not faint, nor is He weary? His understanding is

inscrutable. 29 He gives power to the faint, and to those who have no might, He increases strength.

So just think spiritual stretching strengthens our ability to move freely. Free to follow, to reach, and to press towards the goal. Just think of those times when you get that good stretch in after working long hours or sitting in the same position for too long. Your entire body feels rejuvenated just by you lifting your arms, taking in a deep breath, blowing it out and most likely making a sound of release and renewal.

We all have a journey to follow, it's up to us how we choose to pursue it. I want to suggest that you seek with all diligence. Diligence will show up as a reward. The reward is what happens when we continue to reach for and pursue the goal.

Think of it like an athlete who trains for a race they want the end result to be the first-place prize but guess what they are not just training for one marathon. This means they never stop reaching, they never stop stretching their physical and mental capacity because there is always another race to win. Because we are created to represent the perception of God, we are designed for pursuit. You are built to reach, to grow, to develop fully into being who God has made you to **BE**.

> **1 Peter 2:9 ESV But you are a chosen race, a royal priesthood, a holy nation, a people for his own possession, that you may proclaim the excellences of him who called you out of darkness into his marvelous light.**

My prayer is that this is a reminder that would give a jolt that sticks with us until the end and hoping that every time you feel like you cannot move freely, you will push with a tenaciousness because you have a firm grip on who you is. This makes you press on until you feel the flow of Gods spirit breathing into your **BEING**. Causing light to expose the darkest of places in our lives and the lives of others. When there is light on it, light breathes life and causes the darkness to disappear for good. There is coming a time when there will be resistance and whatever it is, must be pushed out of the way. Move it out immediately. Take away its ability to restrain who you are. What many fail to realize is once the announcement is decreed as you are making your way through the birth canal the law of the universe must give way for us to walk through the journey set for us.

Chapter 13

Remain Resilient

It is on purpose and with the clear intent that whenever you hear me speak or read something I wrote; it will somehow always summons the resilience in us to persevere. To continue pushing and tugging at us no matter what we face. This to me, my friend is as important as breathing that you can "recover (improve) quickly from difficulties," that you have a toughness within (Oxford Dictionary). I am enamored by this definition of what it means to be resilient. First, is having the capacity, indicating being able to embrace the difficulty and it does not consume who you are. Having the ability means your capability is at maximum strength, and we are now able to contain the challenge.

You can bring the pain into captivity. Think of when a firefighter says the fire is contained, I've learned this means the fire is out, it is no longer burning, no longer able to cause damage. Come on get excited here! We are no longer enslaved to troubles. Troubles can no longer cause harm. Yes, problems will come, but they have no power. **Say it out loud, my troubles have no power!** Second, we are not wasting any more time waddling in difficulty as before. We see it, feel it, maybe taste or touch too, but that is it. We no longer sway back and forth. We are now balanced and steady, having an expectation of moving forward quickly being resilient. We can do this because we are no longer numb, we have our feeling back. Our spiritual, physical, and mental senses are working effectively. We are now controlling the difficulty it does not control us. We are conquerors! Always remember you are a winner! I say to always remember because you realize there are more hurdles to jump, more mountains to climb, and more giants to slay. No worries, you got this no opposition/difficulty here that cannot be defeated. Now that our mind has been renewed and restored, we can rightfully claim the provisions of greatness that is alive within us. Rest assuredly, there are more victories to win. Remain steadfast, the journey is not over. There are more books to write, more cakes to bake, more pictures to take, and more love to share. Read 2 Corinthians chapter 10, verses 3 through 6 out loud. Make it your daily affirmation.

2 Corinthians 10:3-6 Message Bible Translation The world is unprincipled. It's dog-eat-dog out there! The world doesn't fight fair. But we don't live or fight our battles that way—never have and never will. The *tools* of our trade aren't for marketing or manipulation, but they are for demolishing that entire massively corrupt culture. We use our powerful God-*tools* for smashing warped philosophies, tearing down barriers erected against the truth of God, fitting every loose thought and emotion and impulse into the structure of life shaped by Christ. Our *tools* are ready at hand for clearing the ground of every obstruction and building lives of obedience into maturity.

Always Remember

My friends if you take away nothing else from the words on these pages. Please still remember you have the tools and the power to accomplish anything you put your mind too. The caveat to this is, your brain – the center of everything within you, must be active and alive so it can provide instructions to your heart and your heart will give instructions to your body and your body will execute the command. You are resilient and can bounce back quickly from any adversity/opposition that comes your way!

Always **BE** Awesome!

No longer bound I am FREE!

Made in United States
North Haven, CT
04 May 2023